THE ACROPOLIS

Caryatids of the Erechtheum; preceding page shows the Battle of Centaurs and Lapithae represented on a Parthenon metope.

THE ACROPOLIS

by MICHITARŌ TANAKA
photographs by
BIN TAKAHASHI

KODANSHA INTERNATIONAL LTD.
TOKYO, NEW YORK & SAN FRANCISCO

Distributors:
UNITED STATES: *Kodansha International/USA, Ltd., through Harper & Row, Publishers, Inc., 10 East 53rd Street, New York, 10022.* SOUTH AMERICA: *Harper & Row, Publishers, Inc., International Department.* CANADA: *Fitzhenry & Whiteside Limited, 150 Lesmill Road, Don Mills, Ontario.* MEXICO AND CENTRAL AMERICA: *HARLA S. A. de C. V., Apartado 30–546, Mexico 4, D. F.* UNITED KINGDOM: *Phaidon Press Limited, Littlegate House, St. Ebbe's Street, Oxford OX1 1SQ.* EUROPE: *Boxerbooks Inc., Limmatstrasse 111, 8031 Zurich.* AUSTRALIA AND NEW ZEALAND: *Book Wise (Australia) Pty. Ltd., 104–8 Sussex Street, Sydney 2000.* THE FAR EAST: *Toppan Company (S) Pte. Ltd., Box 22 Jurong Town Post Office, Jurong, Singapore 22.*

Published by Kodansha International Ltd., 2–12–21 Otowa, Bunkyo-ku, Tokyo 112 and Kodansha International/USA, Ltd., 10 East 53rd Street, New York, New York 10022 and 44 Montgomery Street, San Francisco, California 94104. Copyright © 1969 by Kodansha International Ltd. All rights reserved. Printed in Japan.

LCC 75–82654
ISBN 0–87011–085–3
JBC 0371-780961-2361

First edition, 1969
Fifth printing, 1977

CONTENTS

SACRED CITADEL

THE word *acropolis* in Greek means the topmost part of a city—a fact the visitor to Athens appreciates immediately. Soaring high on a hill above the surrounding rooftops, the Acropolis is the first sight he sees—and the last. Although it was a sacred place, with temples and statues of deities, it had no independent temples to start with.

Like other Greek acropoleis, of which there were a number, that of Athens was first constructed as a citadel, from where the surrounding farmland might be protected and where the people themselves might take refuge in case of invasion. The only access to the Acropolis of Athens is a path on the western side of the hill; the other three sides are steep—and therefore easily defended—cliffs.

As agriculture first began to develop in ancient days, farmers naturally tended to be more sedentary than hunters or shepherds, but at the same time they were obliged to effect some means of protection against incursions by nomadic peoples who, not agriculturalists themselves, envied the fruits of the farmers' year-round labors. A walled and impregnable citadel—an acropolis—was the obvious answer to this life-and-death problem.

THE ACROPOLIS ❧

Many of the world's most ancient city-states, such as those of China, were entirely surrounded by walls, behind which all its citizens dwelt. Even farmers used to live within the walls and to leave them only at dawn in order to tend their fields. But this way of living was not, generally speaking, true of ancient Greece, where large numbers of farmers lived outside the city, and many early Greek city-states originally had no walls at all. Athens became a fortified city only in its later, imperialistic stage of development.

Thus, the citadel—the acropolis—played a very important role, for it was the sole place of refuge available to the citizens in case of invasion. On the other hand, when the walls were built around the whole area of Athens, the whole city was, we may say, turned into an acropolis. Thus, both the strategy of Pericles at the time of the Peloponnesian War and that of Themistocles at the time of the Persian War will be regarded as much the same as that of the first rulers of Athens: all of them were intending to defend the city against attack, relying on the Acropolis as their last resort.

With the completion of the city walls, the significance of the Acropolis became less vital from a military, and more vital from a religious point of view. People continued to lead their daily lives on the lower land surrounding the fortified and sacred hill. At first, since they were exposed to constant attack, they built their houses as high and as close to the Acropolis as they could get—perhaps, as Thucydides suggests, on the southern slope. Then, as time went on, they began to move down. But, as Plato observes in the *Laws*, it takes many years for a people to change its residence from a high land to a low land. Then at last, in the Classical Age, the city of Athens— in Herodotus' figurative description—spread in the shape of a wheel, of which the hub was the Acropolis.

But the hub was, in a sense, a double one—for just below the Acropolis was the Agora, the ever growing center of the life of the people. The history of Athens is, in part, the history of the mutual relationship between the Acropolis and the Agora.

Homer uses the word *agora* to mean both "an assembly of the people" and "the place where an assembly is held." In time it came also to mean "a marketplace." The reasons are obvious: the place where people meet is eminently suited also to be the place where they come to buy and sell, to meet friends, to discuss the affairs of everyday life—probably much like the Roman Forum in its early days.

The Agora of Athens lies just below the north-western slope of the Acropolis and near the northern side of the Areopagus. A path leads to the west entrance of the Acropolis. Originally it was the site for the transaction not only of private but also of public business. Assemblies of all the citizens of Athens were held there. Then, toward the end of the sixth century B.C., public meetings began to be held on the Hill of the Pnyx, beyond the Areopagus. The Pnyx affords a splendid panorama of the Acropolis, and tourists gather there now, on fine summer nights, to view *son et lumière* spectacles, when the Parthenon and the other buildings of the Acropolis are illuminated.

Originally the Agora may also have been the site of athletic events and theatrical performances, but as the city grew it was found to be too small to contain all these diverse activities as well as shops and administrative buildings, so theatres and stadiums were built in other parts of the city. The Agora, nonetheless, remained the heart of the city. A Greek *polis*, or city-state, might exist without walls but not without its *agora*. So integral was it, in fact, in the daily life of the Greeks that, as Plato notes in his *Theaetetus*, a citizen

9

who went there to see a friend would wonder why, when he failed to find him.

In Athens, all roads led to the Agora, and all distances were measured from the Altar of the Twelve Gods that stood in its center. The road from the Agora to the Acropolis was the route by which went the processions during the Panathenaic Festival. This road, if taken in the opposite direction, i.e., to the north-west, leads you through the Dipylon to the Keramikos and the site of Plato's Academy.

As the city grew and its walls now began to rise, they took over the defensive role formerly played by the Acropolis. But, although its military significance now diminished, it was no less important than before in the life of the people, for the ground was sacred to Athena, patron goddess and protectress of the city. Not only was the Acropolis the imperishable symbol of the *polis* called Athens but at the same time it was encircled by the chief meeting-places of the citizens: the Agora was within a stone's throw; just below the southern slope stood the Theatre of Dionysus; nearby rose the Hill of the Pnyx and the Areopagus—the latter the legendary site where Orestes was tried for the murder of his mother. The Acropolis, then, throughout its long history, remained the hub around which the great wheel of Athens turned.

*

The earliest history of the Acropolis, naturally, like that of all ancient sacred places, is shrouded in myth and legend. Homer apparently refers to it twice. In the *Odyssey* he relates how Athena, after having rescued Odysseus, "went away over the sea . . . to Marathon and to the spacious streets of Athens, where she entered

1. *Athena Parthenos*, the city's guardian deity, was enshrined in the Parthenon. Phidias' original statue was in ivory and gold and some thirty feet high; this marble model is in the National Museum of Athens.

2. *Panoramic view* of the Acropolis, taken from the Philopappus Hill. The Acropolis was rebuilt, under Pericles, in less than half a century, after its destruction by the Persians and after Athens had assumed leadership of the Delian League. Below, on the left, is the Odeum of Herodes Atticus, still in use as a theatre today; in the far distance, on the right, rises Mount Lycabettus.

3. *Piraeus*, port of Athens, was connected to the city by the Long Walls, built around 460 B.C. as a protective measure. It became Greece's major port and remains so today, with a present population of about four hundred thousand, including suburbs. The only city in contemporary Greece that is larger is Athens, with a population of around 560,000.

the abode of Erechtheus." The "abode" of Erechtheus, a mythical king of Athens, is thought to have been upon the Acropolis. The *Iliad* also mentions "the strong city of Athens" (the Acropolis) and tells how Erechtheus, Son of the Earth, was brought up by Athena in Athens, "in her own rich sanctuary. There, every year, the youths of Athens worship him with sacrifice of bulls and rams."

Homer does not mention Erichthonius, but the latter also enters the legendary history of Athens, of which he too was a mythical king. It was he, according to some sources, who inaugurated the Panathenaic Festival. One version identifies Erechtheus with Erichthonius, but Apollodorus, in the *Mythology* attributed to him, makes a distinction. His version of the story is that Athena came to Hephaestus to have some armor made, at which Hephaestus, who had been abandoned by his wife Aphrodite, was smitten with love for her. Hephaestus was determined to have her, but Athena, the Virgin Goddess, was equally determined to remain virgin. In the ensuing struggle, Hephaestus' passion overcame him, and his seed fell on Athena's leg. She wiped it off with a bit of wool, which she threw onto the ground, and from the semen that touched the ground was born Erichthonius. (*Eri* in Greek meant "wool"; *chthon*, "earth.") Athena brought him up secretly, without the knowledge of the other gods, and this Erichthonius, according to Apollodorus, became the grandfather of Erechtheus.

Whichever one prefers, Homer's version or Apollodorus', what attracts our attention most is that the goddess Athena is closely related with the city of Athens in both these versions. She was not only protectress of the city and a goddess of both wisdom and war but she also shared with Hephaestus an interest in arts and industries. The present-day visitor to Athens, standing in the Agora, can look

15

THE ACROPOLIS ❦

up to the Parthenon, which was sacred to Athena, and then turn across to a slightly older and far better preserved temple which, although it is called the Theseum, was apparently sacred to Hephaestus. And atop the Acropolis, the Erechtheum enshrined not only Erechtheus but Athena as well.

*

The assumption is generally made that the name of the city was derived from the name of the goddess, and this is probably correct. Certainly the quotation from the *Odyssey* I have given above would seem to bear out the fact that long before written history the goddess Athena was enshrined in the abode of the king of Athens on the Acropolis. However, as to precisely when this momentous event occurred, we remain in doubt. Homer—if he was indeed the author of the *Odyssey*—was singing about events that occurred— if they ever did occur—long before his own time. That Athena became the patron goddess of the city is an indubitable fact, and the *Odyssey* gives proof that the event occurred far back in history, though exactly how far back is unknown.

Herodotus, in his *History*, gives the following account of how Athena vanquished Poseidon.

"In this citadel there is a temple dedicated to Erechtheus—the Earth-born, as he is called—containing an olive tree and a well of seawater. Athenians say that these were placed there by Poseidon and Athena when they contended for the country. Then, when the Persians occupied the place, the olive tree was burnt along with all the rest. However, on the day after its burning, when the Persian king, Xerxes, commanded certain Athenians to offer sacrifices at the temple, they went up there and found a fresh shoot, over a foot long, growing from the old trunk. Such, at any rate, was the account these people gave." (The occupation of the Acropolis that Herodotus refers to is that by the Persians in 480 B.C.)

Apollodorus tells a different story. In early days, he says, gods vied with each other to become patrons of men and secure their reverence—and the two gods who came to Attica were, first, Poseidon and then Athena. Poseidon struck his trident into the midst of the Acropolis, whereupon seawater gushed out, while Athena planted an olive tree (still to be seen in Apollodorus' day). Each deity wanted the possession of certain districts. To break the deadlock, Zeus parted them and selected, as arbitrator between them, (some say) Cecrops, first king of Attica, half-man, half-snake, and born of the earth. Others say it was Cecrops' successor, Cranaus. In fact, says Apollodorus, it was the twelve gods themselves who arbitrated the dispute; they favored Athena because it was she— on the testimony of Cecrops—who first planted an olive tree in Attica. In return, she gave the district her protection—and her name. But Poseidon, furious, caused a flood that covered all of Attica with seawater.

The myth of the contention between the two gods, may be a reflection of a human battle—that between two groups of people regarding the unification of Attica, one group professing reverence for Athena, the other for Poseidon. The name "Erechtheum" was originally applied to only a part of the temple that enshrined Erechtheus as well as the two gods, but later the whole temple came to be called the Erechtheum, as was the case with the Parthenon, which was also originally only a part of the temple. Thus, we seem to have abundant evidence by which to infer that not only Athena but also Poseidon and Erechtheus were connected with the

THE ACROPOLIS 🌱

Acropolis in its earliest days. Relics that have been unearthed tell more about this connection.

*

Cecrops, to judge by early terra-cotta figurines, seems to have been rather like a merman: the upper half of his body was human, and the lower half that of a snake. "The Athenians," Herodotus tells us, "say that in their Acropolis they have a huge serpent that lives in the temple and is guardian of the whole place. Not only did they say this, but every month—as if the serpent really dwelt there—they laid out its food, which consisted of a honey-cake. Up until this time, the honey-cake had always been consumed; but now it remained untouched. When the priestess told the people what had happened, they left Athens more willingly, believing that the goddess had already forsaken the citadel." The temple Herodotus refers to is probably the Erechtheum, where Athena may have been worshiped in the form of a snake, which was one of her attributes.

The snake appears in another of Apollodorus' stories, in which he describes Athena's intention of rearing the earth-born child (Erichthonius) without the other gods knowing about his existence. She therefore put the child into a box, and commanded Pandrosos, one of the daughters of Cecrops, to keep it, enjoining her at the same time never to open the lid of the box. But a sister of Pandrosos secretly opened the mysterious box and there saw the child with a serpent entwined around his body.

As to what happened next, there are several diverging accounts. One says that the serpent bit the sisters and that they died immediately of the bite. Another story has it that Athena, enraged, drove the sisters mad and they committed suicide by throwing themselves down from the height of the Acropolis. In any case, what seems obvious is that if Cecrops was half-snake, his daughters must have been involved with serpents as well, and the earth-born Athenians must also have felt an affinity for snakes. Very likely, a large number of serpents, as well as owls, inhabited the Acropolis; the present-day visitor to the Parthenon ought to bear that in mind—and read Aristophanes' *Lysistrata*.

It is interesting to note in this connection that Phidias' colossal gold-and-ivory statue of Athena in the Parthenon carried a shield, beside which is found a coiled serpent. The fact that a number of extremely ancient snake-goddesses have been unearthed in Crete has led scholars to surmise that perhaps Athena herself was originally one of them and that she came to the Greek mainland from the south. A snake-goddess holding a spear, carved on a ring unearthed at Knossos in Crete, gives added weight to this supposition, since Athena, goddess of war as well as guardian deity of Athens, is often represented in Athenian statuary as holding a spear in her left hand. Some scholars even believe that other goddesses of Greece may be traced back to Crete, perhaps by way of Mycenae.

Thucydides, now no longer in the realm of myth, makes the following assertion in his *History of the Peloponnesian War*:

"It is evident that the country now called Hellas had not until recently a settled population. On the contrary, migrations were of frequent occurrence, the several tribes abandoning their homes under the pressure of superior numbers. Without commerce, without freedom of communication either by land or sea, cultivating no more of their territory than the exigencies of life required, destitute of capital, never planting their land (for they could not tell when an invader might come and take it all away, and when he did come they had no walls to stop him), thinking that the necessities of daily sustenance could be supplied at one place as well as another, they cared little about shifting their habitation, and consequently neither built large cities nor attained to any other form of greatness. The richest soils were always most subject to this change of masters, such as the district now called Thessaly, Boeotia, most of the Peloponnese (Arcadia excepted), and the most fertile parts of the rest of Hellas. The goodness of the land favored the aggrandizement of particular individuals, and thus created faction which proved a fertile source of ruin. It also invited invasion. Accordingly Attica, owing to the poverty of its soil, enjoying from a very remote period freedom from faction, never changed its inhabitants. And here is no inconsiderable exemplification of my assertion that the migrations were the cause of there being no such growth in other parts. The most powerful victims of war or faction from the rest of Hellas took refuge with the Athenians as a safe retreat; and at an early period, becoming naturalized, swelled the already large population of the city to such a height that Attica became at last too small to hold them, and they had to send out colonies to Ionia."

Attica, then, of which Athens was to become the capital, had occupied a unique position in Greek life from very early days—for it alone was exempt from the waves of migration that continually changed the character of other parts of the Balkan Peninsula. Erechtheus and Erichthonius, those first legendary kings of Athens, were said to have been "born of the earth," and the people of Athens, their descendants, made the same claim for themselves. The findings of excavations emphasize the area's indigenous characteristics.

Thucydides also tells us that the Athenians were the first people to give up the habit of carrying arms with them—evidence that the security of the city of Athens was more than adequate. The culture that flourished on the Acropolis was a very old one then, and it received both strength and impetus from the geographical, economic, and political conditions prevailing on the Attic plain.

The "legendary" kings dominated the Acropolis and its southern slope, but very little else: the other *poleis* of Attica were independent, with their own laws and rulers. It was not until the reign of Theseus —who is half-legendary and half-historical—that they were unified, and the city-state of Athens, as we know it today, came into being, with the Acropolis at its center. Many of the people who dwelt in the Attic plain were not inhabitants of Athens but enjoyed Athenian citizenship by being permitted to play a part in administering the new city-state. Here again it is useful to quote Thucydides, who, speaking of the beginning of the Peloponnesian War, when country people were forced to evacuate their farms and move to Athens, tells us:

"But they found it hard to move, as most of them had always been used to live in the country. From very early times this had been more the case with the Athenians than with others. Under Cecrops and the first kings, down to the reign of Theseus, Attica had always consisted of a number of independent townships, each with its own town hall and magistrates. Except in times of danger, the king at Athens was not consulted; in ordinary seasons they carried on their government and settled their affairs without his interference; sometimes they even waged war against him, as in the case of the Eleusinians with Eumolpus against Erectheus. In Theseus, however, they had a king, at once intelligent and powerful. One of the chief features in his organization of the country was to abolish the council-chambers and magistrates of the petty cities, and to merge them in the single council-chamber and town hall of the present capital. Individuals might still enjoy their private property just as before, but they were henceforth compelled to have only one political center—viz., Athens, which thus counted all the inhabitants of Attica among her citizens, so that when Theseus died he left a great state behind him. Indeed, from him starts the Synoecia, or "Feast of Union", which was paid for by the state and which the Athenians still keep in honor of the goddess. Before this, the city consisted of the present citadel and the district beneath it looking rather towards the south."

Thus, the ancient Athens that we know today is the product of this period of unification; very little is known of the earlier period.

*

It is, of course, impossible to fix any accurate time for the reigns of the "legendary" kings—but the unification of Attica, with the consequent emergence of Athens as its capital, must be considered a historical fact; and the migration to Ionia, of which Thucydides speaks, almost certainly took place, too.

Very likely, the ancestors of the ancient Greeks first appeared in the Balkan Peninsula around 2000 B.C., and some eight hundred years later King Agamemnon of Mycenae effected his epic conquest of Troy, by which time the so-called Mycenaean culture had certainly spread to many parts of Greece. The beginnings of the Acropolis may also date from the same period, with the first kings welcoming Athena to their abode.

When, then, did the legendary-historical Theseus accomplish his unification of Attica? Soon after the Trojan War ended, the Dorians invaded Greece, plunging it into confusion and chaos and

22

wholly destroying Mycenaean culture. Thucydides tells us: "Even after the Trojan War, Hellas was still engaged in migrating and settling, and thus could not attain to the quiet which must precede growth. The late return of the Hellenes from Ilium caused many revolutions, and factions ensued almost everywhere; and it was the citizens thus driven into exile who founded the cities. Sixty years after the capture of Ilium, the modern Boeotians were driven out of Arne by the Thessalians. . . . Eighty years later, the Dorians and the Heraclids became masters of the Peloponnese." For a whole century, then, after the Trojan War ended, Greece was subject to waves of migration and to social upheaval. "Many years had to elapse," Thucydides continues, "before Hellas could attain to a durable tranquillity undisturbed by expulsions, and could begin to send out colonies, as Athens did to Ionia and most of the islands, and the Peloponnesians to most of Italy and Sicily and some places in the rest of Hellas. All these places were founded subsequent to the Trojan War."

Greek expansion overseas was in part the result of such warlike expeditions as those to Crete and Troy, in part the result of migratory waves that forced the earlier inhabitants to leave, and in part the result of the natural increase in population. Which was the main factor in this outward expansion, it is impossible to say. Nor is it possible to say whether the Thesean unification was carried out before or after the exodus, but it seems reasonable to suppose that such a unification heralded the close of the "Dark Age" that followed the destruction of the culture of the Trojan War period. The unification of Attica may, to a certain degree, be compared to the unification of Europe by Charlemagne which ended another "Dark Age" that followed the fall of the Roman Empire.

THE ACROPOLIS ✣

Excavations at the Keramikos, in north-west Athens, have brought to light examples of geometrically patterned pottery which are believed to have been manufactured during the time when Athens was the capital of a united Attica. Pottery with geometric patterns is typical of the period from 1000 to 750 B.C.—a particularly important one in the history of the formation of Greek culture.

*

Theseus, if, indeed, he was not a mere legendary figure, may, in unifying Attica, have deprived the lesser rulers of the region of their absolute authority; and the resulting decrease in their prerogatives may also have detracted from his own—although he was a most powerful ruler. We know little about the process that resulted in the gradual shift from monarchy to aristocracy. That the shift, however, was gradual seems obvious, for it was apparently unaccompanied by revolution; real progress can only be attained through a gradual and continuous process, not through mere destruction. The tenure of the chief posts in the aristocracy, originally of life-long duration, was in time reduced to ten years, and later to one year. Even so, citizens who were not members of the ruling class began to resent the power that it held, and Athens, at the dawn of the sixth century B.C., was pregnant with the possibility of civil disorder.

It was then (594 B.C.) that Solon appeared upon the scene—and our knowledge of Athenian life becomes more graphic and more accurate. As arbitrator, Solon took temporary measures cancelling all debts and forbidding free men to offer themselves into slavery as collateral in borrowing money. Most important of all, probably, he promulgated a constitution which has proved itself to be the basis and a model in the history of democratic legislation of the world; even Pisistratus' establishment of a dictatorship (560–527 B.C.) was not an outright violation of its principles.

"Pisistratus," writes Aristotle, in his *Athenian Constitution*, "had the reputation of being an extreme democrat, and he also had distinguished himself greatly in the war with Megara. Taking advantage of this, he wounded himself, and by representing that his injuries had been inflicted on him by his political rivals, he persuaded the people, through a motion proposed by Aristion, to grant him bodyguards. After he got these 'club-bearers,' as they were called, he made an attack with them on the people and seized the Acropolis. This happened in the archonship of Comeas, thirty-one years after the legislation of Solon."

During the dictatorship of Pisistratus—and of his sons, Hippias and Hipparchus—Athens made great strides, both economically and culturally; and the dictators also weakened the power of the nobles, so that by 507 B.C., when the tyrants were expelled under the leadership of Cleisthenes, Athens was already on the way toward democracy. Cleisthenes proclaimed a new, and far more democratic, constitution, with a far broader popular basis for the various legislative, administrative, and judicial bodies of the city-state. Cleisthenes belonged to the illustrious family of the Alcmeonidae, who were later to produce the great Pericles and who had, in the dimmer past, according to Thucydides, expelled another tyrant named Cylon, who had occupied the Acropolis around 630 B.C. and attempted to establish a dictatorship. Cylon himself managed to escape, but his followers, although they begged for their lives at the base of the statue of Athena, were all executed. The Acropolis, during its long history, has been the scene of much bloodshed as well as of peaceful worship of the gods, witness of grief and suffering as well as joy.

Cleisthenes himself was also exiled temporarily, when a rival faction asked for, and obtained, the help of Spartan soldiers in this operation. But the people rebelled, and Cleisthenes' rivals were driven into the Acropolis, where, after two days without food and water, they agreed that Cleisthenes should resume control of the government.

*

About thirty years after Cleisthenes had inaugurated his reforms, the Acropolis was wholly destroyed by fire and pillage. Herodotus tells us that the Persians took a month to cross the Hellespont and then began their three-months' march toward Attica. "Wherever they went, the country was wasted with fire and sword, the cities and even the temples being wilfully set alight by the troops."

Fortunately, the threat of a Persian invasion had brought to the front strong-minded men like Themistocles and Militiades, and it was on Themistocles' advice that the Athenian navy was greatly strengthened, so that the Persians might be routed by sea. The Oracle at Delphi, furthermore, had told the Athenians to defend themselves in "a wooden castle," which many took to be a ship, so that they were prepared to accept Themistocles' advice. A number of Athenians took refuge on the island of Salamis. Some, however, interpreting the Oracle differently, strengthened the Acropolis with wooden paling in an attempt to defend it against the approaching horde of Persians.

The invaders ensconced themselves on the Areopagus, from where they attempted to set fire to the Acropolis by shooting flaming arrows at the wooden palisades. The defenders countered by shooting rocks at the Persians and succeeded, for a time, in warding off the attack—but only for a time.

"At last, however," says Herodotus, "in the midst of these many difficulties, the barbarians made discovery of an access. For verily the Oracle had spoken the truth; it was fated that the whole mainland of Attica should fall beneath the sway of the Persians. Right in front of the citadel, but from behind the gates and common ascent— where no watch was kept, and no one would have thought it possible that any foot of man could climb—a few soldiers mounted from near the sanctuary of Aglaurus, Cecrops' daughter, notwithstanding the steepness of the precipice. As soon as the Athenians saw them upon the summit, some threw themselves headlong from the wall, and so perished; while others fled for refuge to the inner part of the temple. The Persians rushed to the gates and opened them, after which they massacred the suppliants. When all were slain, they plundered the temple, and fired every part of the citadel."

In reply, the Athenians carried out a kind of "scorched earth" policy, in an attempt to free themselves from the Persians, and engaged them in a great sea battle, which ended in victory for the Greeks. The following year, in the Battle of Plataea, the combined Greek forces routed the remnants of the Persian invaders. The final result was total victory for the Greeks. The Athenian navy took control of the Aegean Sea, and Athens, assuming hegemony over the other city-states of Greece, started on its imperial path.

Thucydides says that "the Athenian people, after the departure of the barbarian from their country, at once proceeded to carry over their children and wives, and such property as they had left, from the places where they had deposited them, and prepared to rebuild their city and their walls. For only isolated portions of the circumference had been left standing, and most of the houses were in ruins, though a few remained, in which the Persian grandees had taken up their quarters."

Despite Spartan protests, Themistocles now began construction of a great wall around Athens and later the famous long walls that led to the port of Piraeus. It was these walls that enabled the Athenians to live, for the first time, in safety by the sea; to cast their eyes seawards, and ultimately to build an empire.

Defensive walls and housing took precedence over reconstruction of the Acropolis. It was not really until the rise to power of Pericles (443–429 B.C.) that the great temples, whose ruins are so familiar to us today, were erected. Presumably the Parthenon was constructed between 447 and 438, the Propylaea between 437 and 432, the Temple of Athena Nike between 426 and 421, and the Erechtheum between 421 and 406. The workmen, Plutarch tells us, in his *Life of Pericles*, strove "to outvie the material and the design with the beauty of their workmanship, yet the most wonderful thing of all was the rapidity of their execution. Undertakings, any one of which might singly have required, they thought, for their completion, successions and ages of men, were accomplished in the height and prime of one man's political service."

Plutarch lived from about the latter half of the first century to the beginning of the second century A.D., more than half a millennium after the completion of the Acropolis; yet, he continues, "Pericles' works are admired especially for this: they were achieved in a very short time, and yet have stood firm for a very long period. For every piece of his work was even at that time, antique for its beauty and elegance, and yet, in its vigor and freshness, looks to this day as if it were just executed. There is a sort of bloom of newness upon those works of his, preserving them from the touch of time, as if they had some perennial spirit and vitality mingled in the composition of them."

Plutarch notes also that Pericles' rehabilitation of the Acropolis had political and economic as well as religious motives behind it. (Present-day governments are similarly motivated.) In his *Life of Pericles*, Plutarch writes:

"With a variety of workmanship and of occasions for service, which summon all arts and trades and require all hands to be employed about them, they do actually put the whole city, in a manner, into state pay; while, at the same time, she is both beautified and maintained by herself. . . .

"Those who are of age and strength are rewarded in many ways by the state for their service rendered at times of war, while others, such as underservants, who have not served in the army, go without their share of the public salaries. Pericles thought it a pity, but he also thought that they should not be paid for nothing. It is through these considerations that he dared to propose to the Assembly the tremendous project of the reconstruction of the Acropolis, which would require a vast amount of art and time. It was to give opportunities to enjoy the public welfare to those who stay at home as well as to those who undergo military service at sea, in garrisons, or on expeditions.

"The materials were stone, brass, ivory, gold, ebony, cypress-wood; and the arts that wrought and fashioned them were of smiths and carpenters, molders, founders and braziers, stonecutters, dyers, goldsmiths, ivory-workers, painters, embroiderers, turners; those again that conveyed the materials to the town for use, merchants and mariners and ship-masters by sea; and by land, cart-wrights, cattle-breeders, waggoners, rope-makers, flax-workers, shoe-makers and leather-dressers, road-makers, miners. And every trade in the same nature, as a general in the army has his company of soldiers under him, had its own hired company of untrained laborers. Thus, to say all in a word, the occasions and services of these public works distributed plenty among people of every age and condition."

Pericles' aim, then, in instituting these vast public works was to provide total employment for all the citizens of free and democratic Athens—quite unlike the projects of autocratic states that used slaves as forced labor. Athens, at the time, ensured freedom of speech for all, and, as is always seen in a democratic society, there was no lack of vociferous objection to the government's policy.

The huge amounts of money required for these vast projects were provided through the Delian League, which was formed after the rout of the Persians to protect the country against further incursions from the east. The "combined" navy of the Delian League was in fact largely Athenian, though it was financed by funds supplied by other member-states, who found it advantageous to assist Athens to arm herself in order to defend the rest of the country. It was these "membership fees" that Pericles spent in the reconstruction of the Acropolis.

For this he was criticized by opposition parties, who claimed it was an "appropriation of the funds" that would discredit Athens in the eyes of her allies. Pericles' reply, which seems reasonable, was that so long as he made full use of the funds for defense, he was free to use the rest of the money as he pleased—and this decision of his was endorsed by public vote. The reconstruction of the

Acropolis was not made at the command of an autocrat but through discussions in the Assembly. The Acropolis we see today is the result of those discussions.

*

To our regret, however, time and man's destructive nature have left us but a skeleton of the original structures. Throughout these twenty-four hundred years, the Acropolis has been plundered by many different hands. At the close of their Imperial Age, the Romans, who had occupied Greece, carted off innumerable pieces of sculpture, while the Christians, later, destroyed what was left in iconoclastic fervor. They also transformed both the Parthenon and the Erechtheum into Christian churches, destroying much of the interiors in the process and defacing the exteriors. During the Middle Ages, Crusaders and Florentine adventurers further remodelled the Parthenon and turned the Propylaea into a palace, effecting profound structural changes in the entire complex. Later still, the Moslems transformed the Parthenon into a mosque and used the Erechtheum as general headquarters for the Arab forces. The Temple of Athena Nike was demolished by the Turks, who constructed a battery on the site and also used the Parthenon as an arsenal. In 1687, the Venetians, besieging the city, fired at the Parthenon, and the resulting explosions all but destroyed what little was left. Later still, Lord Elgin carried off the famous marbles to England.

What remained has now been painstakingly reconstructed— and the present-day visitor to the Acropolis, though he will see nothing like the splendor that Pausanius saw in the second century and so graphically described in his books on Greece, will nonetheless be strangely moved and awed by the glory of the ruins. The temples

THE ACROPOLIS 🌿

stand empty now, and the marble columns are cracked and defaced, but the pure rationality of the buildings, so integral to all Greek art, science, and philosophy, is still perceptible. Studying the ruins, one realizes that their simple beauty is the result of long and careful planning. Though the temples were built of stone, not wood, the Japanese visitor to the Acropolis sees in them much that reminds him of the simplicity and beauty of the shrines his own ancestors constructed long ago.

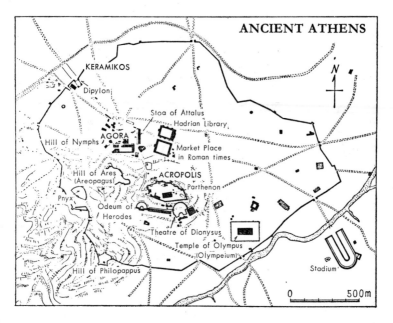

ANCIENT ATHENS

KERAMIKOS
Dipylon
Stoa of Attalus
Hadrian Library
Hill of Nymphs
AGORA
Market Place
in Roman times
Hill of Ares
(Areopagus)
ACROPOLIS
Pnyx
Parthenon
Odeum of
Herodes
Theatre of Dionysus
Temple of Olympus
(Olympeium)
Hill of Philopappus
Stadium

0   500m

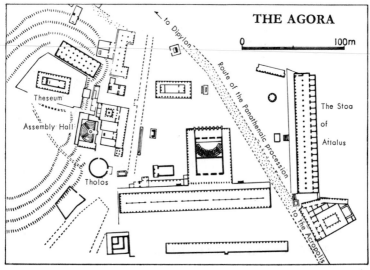

THE AGORA

to Dipylon

0   100m

Theseum

Assembly Hall

Route of the Panathenaic procession

The Stoa
of
Attalus

Tholos

to the ACROPOLIS

MAP OF ANCIENT GREECE

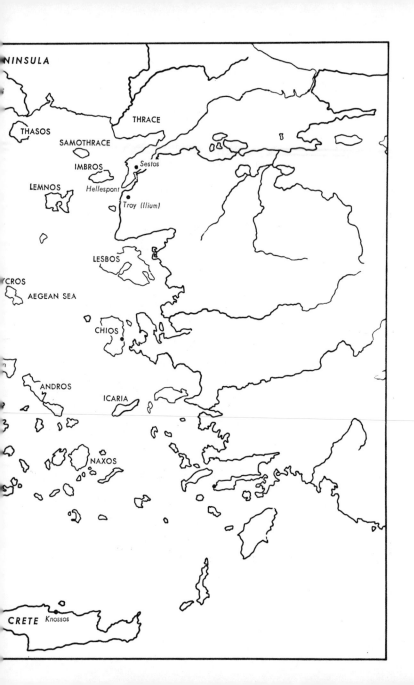

THE ACROPOLIS

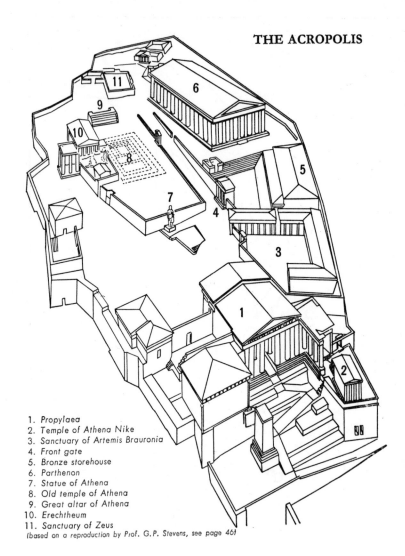

1. Propylaea
2. Temple of Athena Nike
3. Sanctuary of Artemis Brauronia
4. Front gate
5. Bronze storehouse
6. Parthenon
7. Statue of Athena
8. Old temple of Athena
9. Great altar of Athena
10. Erechtheum
11. Sanctuary of Zeus
(based on a reproduction by Prof. G.P. Stevens, see page 46)

THE PARTHENON

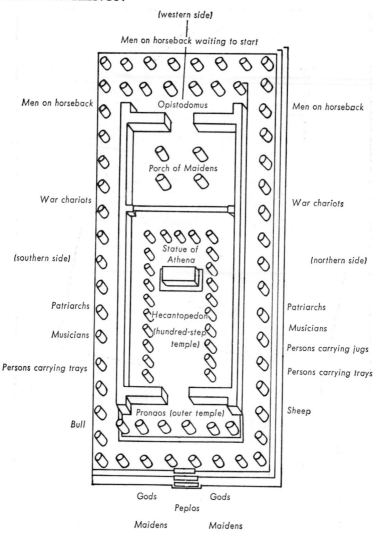

(western side)

Men on horseback waiting to start

Men on horseback

Opistodomus

Men on horseback

Porch of Maidens

War chariots

War chariots

(southern side)

Statue of Athena

(northern side)

Patriarchs

Hecantopedon

Patriarchs

Musicians

(hundred-step temple)

Musicians

Persons carrying jugs

Persons carrying trays

Persons carrying trays

Sheep

Pronaos (outer temple)

Bull

Gods   Gods

Peplos

Maidens   Maidens

(eastern side)

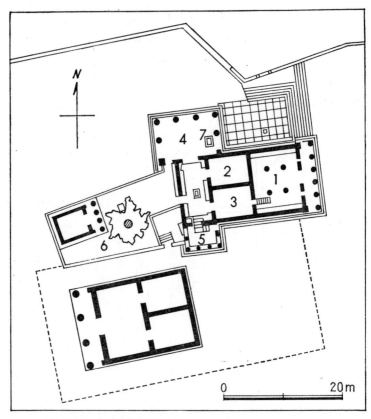

THE ERECHTHEUM

1. *Sanctuary of Athena*   2 and 3. *Sanctuary of Erechtheus and Poseidon*

4. *Porch*   5. *Porch of Caryatids*   6. *Sanctuary of Pandrosos*

7. *Place struck by Poseidon's trident*

(the dotted line encloses the old temple of Athena)

4. *Massive columns* of the Temple of Olympian Zeus, completed by the Roman emperor, Hadrian, around 130 A.D. Fifteen of the original Corinthian columns remain; in the background may be seen the Parthenon.

5. *Entrance* to the Acropolis (on the right) as seen
from the Areopagus; beyond the Propylaea, on
the extreme right, stands the small temple of
Athena Nike. In classical times this was the only

means of access to the Acropolis (and remains so today); the other sides are steep, well-nigh inaccessible cliffs.

6. *Plutarch* writes: "There is a sort of bloom of newness upon those works of Pericles, preserving them from the touch of time, as if they had some perennial spirit and vitality mingled in the composition of them."

7. *Temple of Athena Nike* (far right) with the Propylaea, which were constructed in about five years, beginning in 437, by the architect Mnesicles out of Pentelic marble. North wing was originally decorated with the famous painting of Polygnotus. Damaged in the explosion of 1645, the columns have been re-erected as nearly like the original as possible.

44

8. *Model of Acropolis* as it was during early Roman Period (constructed by the American archaeologist, Prof. G. P. Stevens).

9. *South wing* of Propylaea is smaller than the north wing, perhaps because of its proximity to the extremely small temple of Athena Nike.

10. *West facade* of Parthenon, showing the eight Doric columns of Pentelic marble. Sides have seventeen columns, making forty-six in all, since corner columns are counted twice.

11. *Columns* of Parthenon are slightly ▶ convex, to correct the illusion of concavity, and turn slightly inward, so as to seem more stable.

13—14. *Interior* of Parthenon: six Doric columns marked the entrance to the pronaos; within the naos itself, at the far end, stood the famous monumental statue of Athena Parthenos. Beyond was a room used as a treasury.

52

15—16. *East façade* of the Parthenon, with the corners of the pediment still remaining. According to Pausanias, the figures represented the birth of Athena. Many of them were brought by Lord Elgin to England, where they are now in the British Museum. The sculptures in the corner, shown in Plate 16, are copies.

17—18. *West frieze (see previous page),* in the interior above the walls of the cella, depicted the Panathenaic procession. Shown here are soldiers waiting for the procession to start.

19—20. *Figures* in the left corner of
the east pediment depict Dionysus,
Persephone and Demeter, with (possibly) Artemis. The three goddesses on
the right, two being identified as Leto,
Dione, and the other as Aphrodite,
were presumably watching the birth of
Athena, who sprang full-armed from
the head of Zeus, in the center of the
pediment. (British Museum, London.)

21. *Two goddesses*, perhaps Dione and her daughter Aphrodite, are a perfect example of the subtlety with which Greek sculptors expressed the relation between body and dress. (British Museum, London.)

22. *Artemis* (?), a figure from the left half of the pediment, seems to have been running away from the center. (British Museum, London.)

23. *Leto* (?), sitting figure on the right half, has also been identified as Hestia, goddess of the hearth. (British Museum, London.)

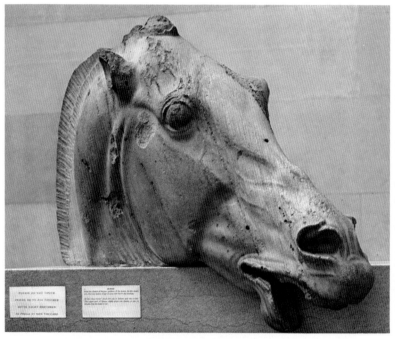

24. *Horse* of Selene, the moon-god-
dess, at the right corner of the east
pediment, as she sank behind the
waves of the sea. At left, the sun-god
began his ascent into the sky. (British
Museum, London.)

25. *Figure* from west pediment tenta-▶
tively identified as Iris, the rainbow-
goddess. The west pediment depicted
the contest between Athena and
Poseidon for possession of Attica.
(British Museum, London.)

◄26. *Three gods* (*see previous page*)—
Poseidon, Apollo, and his sister
Artemis—from the frieze on the
eastern wall of the cella, waiting for
the arrival of the Panathenaic proces-·
sion. The work is attributed to Alca-
menes, pupil of Phidias. (Acropolis
Museum, Athens.)

27. *Artemis*—detail from Plate 26.
(Acropolis Museum, Athens.)

28. *Apollo*—detail from Plate 26. (Acropolis Museum, Athens.)

29. *Bull* being led to sacrifice in the Panathenaic procession, from the north frieze of the Parthenon. Only a few fragments of the frieze remain *in situ* today; most are now in the Acropolis Museum, the British Museum, and the Louvre. Bull shown below is in the Acropolis Museum.

30. *Sheep* for sacrifice meekly follow the recalcitrant bull; face of the youth, though damaged, plainly shows his rustic origin. (Acropolis Museum, Athens.)

31. *Group of maidens*, with two youths, at the beginning of the Panathenaic procession reach the place where the gods are waiting. (Louvre, Paris.)

32. *Youths* carrying some similarly shaped water-jugs, from the north frieze, wear differently draped robes. (Acropolis Museum, Athens.)

33. *Chariots* in the Panathenaic procession; warriors would leap in and out of the chariots as they proceeded. (Acropolis Museum, Athens.)

35. *Captain* issuing commands to mounted soldiers. (Acropolis Museum, Athens.)

36. *Procession* begins at the south-
west corner of the Parthenon, one
section going along the northern wall,
the other along the south; waiting
gods are on the east wall.

37. *Soldiers* go riding in the procession, without either saddle or stirrup, making it difficult for them to control their mounts. (Acropolis Museum, Athens.)

38. *Erechtheum,* in the distance, work on which was begun in 421, was not completed till the year 406. It stands to the north of the Parthenon and was dedicated to the legendary king, Erechtheus, said to have been reared by Athena.

39. *East facade* of the Erechtheum▶ originally had six very elegant Ionic columns, of which one is now in the British Museum. First room was dedicated to Athena Polias, guardian deity.

40. *Caryatids* that sustained the famous porch, six in all, four in the front row and two in the second, at either end. Second from left is a copy.

41. *Original* is in the British Museum. ▶ The women stand comfortably, one leg slightly bent, to suggest that the weight of the roof is not excessive. (British Museum, London.)

◀42. *Temple of Athena Nike* is only 27 by 18½ feet; total height, to tip of now lost pediment, was 23 feet. East frieze, shown here, depicted the gods around Athena.

43. *Architect* of Temple of Athena Nike is said to have been Callicrates; the temple, though small, took thirty years to build.

44—45. *Parapet*, no longer standing, around the temple depicted winged Victories worshiping Athena (*see previous page*); figures are full of action and draperies are beautifully executed. (Acropolis Museum, Athens.)

46. *Persians* attacked and occupied the Acropolis in 480 B.C., tearing down the temples, burning and destroying what they could. Many of these pre-Periclean sculptures have recently been excavated and are now in the collection of the Acropolis Museum. Shown below is a fragment of a pediment, done around the beginning of the sixth century, depicting Hercules' driver with a war chariot. (Acropolis Museum, Athens.)

47. *Lion's head*, which served as a
water spout, at the ancient temple of
Athena during the latter half of the
sixth century. Colors still remain.
(Acropolis Museum, Athens.)

48. *Bull* being clawed by lions (detail)
from a pediment of the ancient temple
of Athena, around the latter half of
the sixth century. Here again, the
colors covering the soft limestone are
plainly visible. (Acropolis Museum,
Athens.)

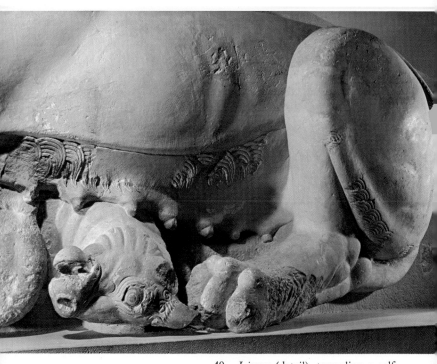

49. *Lioness* (detail), trampling a calf with her paws, is about to devour it. The face of the lioness has been largely lost. (Acropolis Museum, Athens.)

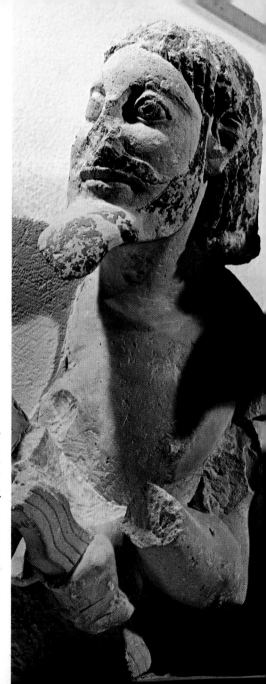

50. *Three-bodied monster* (detail) from a pediment of the first half of the sixth century. Generally thought to be Neleus, a god of the sea, lower half of the monster (not shown) is a coiled serpent. Figure at far right holds a bird; center figure, a river; and that on left, a flame. Beards are colored deep blue. (Acropolis Museum, Athens.)

51—52. *Calf-bearer* may have been the donor of the statue himself, whose name, from an inscription on the base, was something like Bombos, Rhombos, or Kombos. Presumably he was bringing the calf as an offering to Athena. The missing eye-balls were almost certainly made of a different material from the rest of the statue. (Acropolis Museum, Athens.)

53. *Marble sphinx*, with a girl's head and the body of a winged lion, was made around the year 530 B.C. Legend says the monster was anthropophagous, but the face is lovely, with an archaic smile. (Acropolis Museum, Athens.)

54. *Owl* was a symbol of Athena and sacred to her. This figure, made around the beginning of the fifth century, stood on a high pedestal near the sanctuary of Artemis Brauronia, on the west edge of the Acropolis. (Acropolis Museum, Athens.)

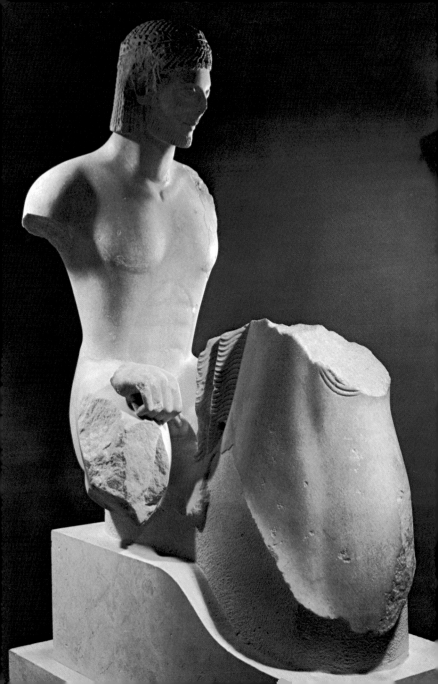

55—56. *Man on horseback*, made of Parian marble around the year 560 B.C. The head in Plate 55 is a copy of the original, which is in the Louvre (shown below). Characteristically archaic, it has the "archaic smile," and stylized beard and hair, adorned with an ivy wreath. (Acropolis Museum, Athens; Louvre, Paris.)

57. *Crouching dog*, which kept watch at the entrance to a temple, dates from around 520 B.C. (Acropolis Museum, Athens.)

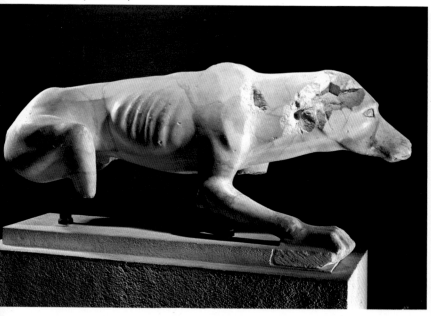

58. *Two horses* (detail), in extremely ▶ high relief, are the central pair of a team of four that pulled a chariot. About 570 B.C. (Acropolis Museum, Athens.)

59. *Kore*, from around the end of the sixth century, is not a typical archaic maiden; expression suggests she may have been intended to represent a goddess. (Acropolis Museum, Athens.)

60. *Relief sculpture*, from around the end of the sixth century, shows three maidens dancing, with Hermes, in the lead, playing a flute. (Acropolis Museum, Athens.)

107

61—62. *Kore* is the name commonly given to special type of standing, archaic Greek sculpture of young girls. The *kore* is robed, while the *kouros* (her male counterpart) is usually nude. This figure dates from around 530 B.C. (Acropolis Museum, Athens.)

63. *Simply robed kore* wearing chiton (*see previous page*). About 510 B.C. (Acropolis Museum, Athens.)

64. *Himation* worn over chiton is brightly colored (*see previous page*); marble is from island of Chios. About 510 B.C. (Acropolis Museum, Athens.)

65. *Style* of beautifully made *kore* below indicates Attica as her place of origin. Around 500 B.C. (Acropolis Museum, Athens.)

66. *Kore*, dedicated by Euthydikos, whose name is inscribed on the base, no longer displays the archaic smile. Attic work, around 490 B.C. (Acropolis Museum, Athens.)

67. *Ionian influence* may be seen in the tranquillity of the pose of *kouros* below. About 490 B.C. (Acropolis Museum, Athens.)

68. *Kouros* opposite stands with his body weight on the left leg and with his left hip drawn slightly inward. Pose seems more relaxed than many other contemporary *kouroi*. About 485 B.C. (Acropolis Museum, Athens.)

69. *When excavated,* this youth had golden hair; no longer archaic, his expression betrays the new tendency toward greater spirituality in Greek art. Attic work around 480 B.C. (Acropolis Museum, Athens.)

70. *Face of youth* (below) is presumed to be work of the Phidian school, around the middle of the fifth century, and is characteristic of the Classical Age. (Acropolis Museum, Athens.)

71—72. *Athena* (detail below), leaning upon her spear, wears a Doric-style peplos, but her helmet is in the Corinthian mode. The block at right may possibly be a gravestone (which would account for the sorrowful expression on the face of the goddess), but it may also be a landmark. Relief sculpture from around the middle of the fifth century. (Acropolis Museum, Athens.)

73. *The Agora* was more than merely a market-place: it became the political, economic, and cultural center of the city and, as such, was an indispensable part of Athenian daily life. It extended over a large square just below the Acropolis to the northwest. The history of Athens may be regarded as the history of the relationship between the

Acropolis and the Agora. Chief landmarks in the panoramic view below are the reconstructed Stoa of Attalus (see Pl. 78), at the extreme right, with a small Byzantine church just across the path, and in the left background the so-called Theseum, best-preserved of all Greek temples in Greece.

74. *Temple of Olympian Zeus*, viewed here from above, was completed by the Roman emperor Hadrian, around 130 A.D. It enshrined a colossal chryselephantine statue of Zeus; fifteen Corinthian columns still remain.

75. *Cave* in Acropolis wall (now a Christian shrine) with two columns above, erected in the Roman Age, and used as pedestals to hold cups donated by victors in choral competitions.

76. *Statue of Hadrian* was erected in the Agora around the second century A.D. In the background, atop the Acropolis wall, stands the Erechtheum.

77. *Remains* of several memorial statues have been excavated recently in the Agora. Torso shown in the plate on the right is of the Roman Period. Above may be seen the Propylaea and the Temple of Athena Nike.

78. *Stoa of Attalus* was originally
built around the year 150 B.C. by Attalus II, King of Pergamum, and was
reproduced in 1953–56 to house the
Agora Museum. In foreground are the
remains of the central stoa. (A stoa is
a portico or covered colonnade.)

79. *Theseum*, the name given because the exploits of Theseus are sculptured on the frieze and metopes, was originally sacred to the god Hephaestus. This Doric temple, slightly older than the Parthenon, stands at the western end of the Agora (see Plate 73)

127

80—81. *Theater of Dionysus,* in its present form, dates from the Roman Period, although plays were performed on the site as early as the fifth century B.C. Shown in the plate on the right are the special seats in the front row, built of Pentelic marble, which were reserved for civic and religious dignitaries. Below is a Silenus from the front of the stage.

82. *Theater of Dionysus* had a seating capacity of more than ten thousand. The semi-circular orchestra in the center was where the chorus danced and sang, with the elevated stage just behind.

83. *Keramikos (see overleaf)*, a district ▶ in the northwest part of ancient Athens, was used as a cemetery from the Mycenaean Age through the Classical Period. Most of the tombstones that have been excavated date from around the fourth century B.C.

84. *Most important* of the Keramikos tombstones have been transferred to the National Museum, and those now to be seen *in situ* are copies. That on the left (below), is presumed to date from the end of the fifth century B.C.

THIS BEAUTIFUL WORLD